faithgirlz

101 THINGS EVERY GIRL SHOULD KNOW

XPERT
DVICE
N STUFF BIG
ND SMALL

From the Editors of Faithgirlz and *Girls' Life* magazine

Other books in the growing Faithgirlz™ library

NONFICTION

Best Party Book Ever!
Big Book of Quizzes
Redo Your Room

Faithgirlz! Handbook
Faithgirlz! Journal
Food, Faith and Fun, Faithgirlz! Cookbook

DEVOTIONALS

Finding God In Tough Times
No Boys Allowed
What's a Girl to Do?
Girlz Rock
Chick Chat
Real Girls of the Bible
God's Beautiful Daughter
Whatever!
Girl Politics
Everybody Tells Me to be Myself But I Don't Know Who I Am
You! A Christian Girl's Guide to Growing Up

BIBLES

NIV Faithgirlz! Bible
NIV Faithgirlz! Backpack Bible

BIBLE STUDIES

Secret Power of Love
Secret Power of Joy
Secret Power of Goodness
Secret Power of Grace

FICTION

The Samantha Sanderson Series
Samantha Sanderson at the Movies (Book One)
Samantha Sanderson on the Scene (Book Two)
Samantha Sanderson Off the Record (Book Three)

The Good News Shoes
Riley Mae and the Rock Shocker Trek (Book One)
Riley Mae and the Ready Eddy Rapids (Book Two)
Riley Mae and the Sole Fire Safari (Book Three)

From Sadie's Sketchbook
Shades of Truth (Book One)
Flickering Hope (Book Two)
Waves of Light (Book Three)
Brilliant Hues (Book Four)

The Girls of Harbor View
Girl Power
Take Charge
Raising Faith
Secret Admirer

Boarding School Mysteries
Vanished (Book One)
Betrayed (Book Two)
Burned (Book Three)
Poisoned (Book Four)

Check out www.faithgirlz.com

ZONDERKIDZ

101 Things Every Girl Should Know
Copyright © 2015 Red Engine, LLC

Requests for information should be addressed to:
Zonderkidz, 3900 *Sparks Drive SE, Grand Rapids, Michigan 49546*

ISBN 978-0-310-74619-5

Done in association with Red Engine, LLC, Baltimore, MD.

Zonderkidz is a trademark of Zondervan.

Editors: Jacque Alberta and Karen Bokram
Contributor: Katie Abbondanza
Cover and interior design: Chun Kim

Printed in China

15 16 17 18 19 20 /DSC/ 10 9 8 7 6 5 4 3 2 1

Consider this collection of 101 pieces of expert advice and insider info your guide to staying happy and sane. In some ways, it's all about the little things: the trick to drinking more water ('cause you know it's good for your body and that it will make your skin glow) to the secret to leaving the perfect note in a classmate's yearbook (trust us: they'll forget that random text you sent, but will sooo look back on that inscription in 20 years). We've also got you covered with study tips (we're seeing more A's in your future), smart ways to chill out (psst: you deserve to relax on the daily) and how to be your awesome, composed self at school and parties alike (hello, confidence). Before you know it, all your friends will be asking how you managed to boost your grades/land such shiny hair/make the JV team. Hey, we'll keep your secret (flip to #8 for a no-fail way to zip those lips)...but it's always sweet to share.

— the editors

SHOP THE THRIFT STORE LIKE A PRO

Whether you're at Goodwill or the Salvation Army, you gotta get creative when sifting through the piles. Here's how to find vintage gold among the duds…

1 **Look for pieces that have potential.** A tailor could easily make too-long pants fit perfectly. A missing button or wonky zipper can probably be repaired. Or you could take scissors to a pair of thrift-store jeans and make 'em into cutoffs.

2 **Be wary of the rose-colored glasses.** If something is stained, badly damaged or genuinely too big (like a jacket or shoes), it's best to just say no. There are also some items that don't quite translate once they've been worn. Think: bikinis. We'll pass, thanks.

3 **Ignore the number.** Remember that sizes from back in the day are different from now. Don't get caught up in the tag. If it sorta looks like it might fit, try it on.

LOVE IT!

The easiest way to try out vintage? Accessories! Major necklaces, silk scarves, kitschy clutches and bejeweled bracelets are all super easy to find (and wear). They'll put a clever twist on your best outfits.

let's go for a ride

LEARN TO LOVE
EXERCISE

I t seems like one of life's great mysteries: Some girls just LOVE to work out while others would rather floss their teeth with barbed wire than hit the gym. Well, guess what? We're here to tell you that even the biggest sweat-phobes can find a routine they heart.

THINK FAST: What was your favorite way to be active when you were teeny? Did you love gymnastics or ballet or just bouncing around the house to whatever song came on? Try yoga or Pilates or Zumba. Was hopscotch your thing? Jump some rope for a mega calorie torcher. Were you more into team sports? Sign up for a rec league or a class at the Y to advance your skills. If you've always been more of a pick-daisies than kick-balls kind of girl, start doing nature walks with your friends. That counts, too.

Once you're back to moving and grooving in a way you enjoy, build from there. It's the rare person who absolutely loves intense cardio or strength training from the start, but try adding in one day of something different and challenging to your weekly routine, like lifting light weights, jogging around the block or taking a bike ride. Variety is key for getting in shape and, over time, we bet you'll appreciate the added strength and energy working out brings. Promise.

2

3

GRACIOUSLY ACCEPT A COMPLIMENT

Lots of chicas find themselves flustered if someone tosses sweet words their way. Pretty? Nah, it's just the dress. Smart? Not it. The next time someone praises you or your abilities, look them in the eyes and simply say, "thank you." It'll be tough at first, but over time you'll learn to embrace the sunshine.

Thank you!

READ ALOUD IN CLASS

Does every time you have to speak in class feel like a public flogging? Usually, when girls feel this way, they just have a serious case of self-consciousness. So here's how you can ease read-out-loud anxiety attacks.

Start by reading aloud at home. Yes, you may feel a little silly reciting Shakespeare to your goldfish, but the idea is to get comfortable with hearing yourself. Then the next time you're in class and get called on, imagine it's just you and Goldie and push forward. Be sure to breathe—many people unconsciously hold their breath when they're nervous, and lack of oxygen just makes you feel even more scared.

And take your time; you're not in a speed-reading contest. The more nervous you are, the more you'll rush. And the more you rush, the more you'll mess up, making you more nervous, and so on. The truth is, most of your classmates are probably daydreaming anyway. Don't be afraid to go at a pace that seems a little slow to you. We bet it's just right.

LOVE IT!

Once you're kinda-sorta comfy reading out loud, start being the first to volunteer. It sounds a little crazy, but raising your hand means there are no surprises. You read when ya want, and then you're d-o-n-e, which just so happened to be the point in the first place.

COOK A TASTY DINNER

We think everyone should have a few dishes they totally slam dunk. Here's the deal: Knowing how to whip up pasta carbonara or roasted chicken means you get to show some love to your friends and fam when they need it. Plus, making meals is a neat little act of self-sufficiency, which will save you loads of moolah in the long run and impress your buds, well, forever.

Cooking is about getting organized, following the directions and going for it. So next time Mom is stirring her signature casserole, watch and take notes. Or scour the web or your family's cookbook collection for mega inspiration. Not sure where to start? This roast chicken is a no-fail, and an essential for every cook-in-training.

LEMON-GARLIC ROAST CHICKEN *(serves 4)*

Our good friend Anne Vassal shared this recipe with us ages ago, and we've been making it ever since. *NOTE: If you don't have a roasting rack, place the chicken on a bed of baby carrots—they'll be delish when the bird is done.*

- 1 (4–5 lbs) roaster chicken, preferably naturally raised
- Olive oil
- 1 large lemon
- 6 large garlic cloves
- A few sprigs of fresh rosemary or thyme, or both
- Kosher or coarse salt
- Freshly ground pepper

5

1 Preheat oven to 400°. Remove the liver packet from the inside of the chicken. Wash the chicken with cold water and pat dry with paper towels. Smear some olive oil onto the bottom of a large baking or roasting pan. Put the chicken on the meat rack, if you have it. Otherwise, place the chicken in the middle of the pan. Smear the olive oil all over the chicken's skin.

2 Wash the lemon and cut it in half, then into 1" pieces. Smash the garlic cloves with the side of a knife, pointing the blade away from your body. No need to remove the garlic skins first. Stuff the chicken with lemons, garlic and herbs. Sprinkle salt and pepper over the chicken. Wash your hands and all surfaces before preparing any other food.

3 Place the chicken in the oven and roast for 1 hour and 15 minutes. With oven mitts on, carefully (remember: it's pretty heavy) remove pan from the oven. Stick the meat thermometer* into the thickest part of the breast. The breast should read 160° with the juices running clear. If you check the dark meat, it should read 180°. If it isn't done, return pan to the oven for another 10 minutes, then check again. Let the chicken rest on the top of the stove for 10 minutes before slicing.

4 **IMPORTANT:** Have an adult assist you in carving the bird. Carve the chicken in the pan so you can save the juices. First, cut the thighs away from the breast, keeping the blade pointed away from your fingers and body. Next, slice the breast into quarter-inch slices. Place the meat on a platter as you slice.

TO SERVE: Smear the roasted garlic on some thick bread. Serve with potatoes and carrots or tossed salad. So good!

TOOLS
- Large baking or roasting pan with meat rack
- Cutting board
- Carving knife, chef knife
- Instant-read meat thermometer*
- Platter

*An instant-read thermometer is an inexpensive, small thermometer that you insert into the thickest part of the meat for an "instant read." Give it a minute to climb to get an accurate reading.

...AND SERVE UP A SIGNATURE DESSERT

6

Bringing homemade sweets to a party will make you an insta fave, plus it's nice to send over a sheet of brownies if someone's not feeling well or your BFF has just been dumped (everyone knows chocolate helps). Here, friend of *GL* Anne Vassal shares her way delicious, secretly vegan (!) cake recipe with us. Hint: check the pantry for ALL the ingredients before ya start.

MAKE-YA-SMILE CHOCOLATE CAKE

- 1 ½ cups sifted, unbleached white flour or whole wheat pastry flour
- ¾ cup sugar
- ⅓ cup unsweetened cocoa powder, sifted
- 1 teaspoon baking soda
- ⅓ cup canola oil
- 1 cup cold water
- 1 tablespoon apple cider vinegar
- 1 teaspoon vanilla

FOR SAUCE

- ½ cup chocolate chips
- About 3 tablespoons vanilla soy milk (the refrigerated, creamy kind) or reduced-fat milk (but not skim milk)

TOOLS

• 8" or 9" square baking pan, or a 9" round cake pan
• Large mixing bowl
• Glass measuring cup, measuring cups, spoons
• Electric mixer
• Rubber spatula
• Wire rack (optional)
• Serrated knife

FOR SAUCE

• Small saucepan
• Measuring cups
• Rubber spatula, whisk

1 Preheat oven to 350°. Lightly oil the bottom of an 8" or 9" baking pan. In a large bowl, combine flour, sugar, cocoa powder, baking soda and salt.

2 Pour in the oil, water, vinegar and vanilla. Using an electric mixer, beat on medium speed until the batter is just blended. You may have to scrape down the batter on the sides of the bowl with a rubber spatula and mix again.

3 Place the pan in the center of the oven and bake for 35–40 minutes or until a toothpick inserted into the center of the cake comes out clean. (A 9" pan will take about 30 minutes.) Remove from the oven immediately and cool on a wire rack for at least 30 minutes before serving. If you want, top it with the sauce below. Drizzle the sauce on before serving.

 In a small saucepan, heat the chocolate chips over very low heat, stirring often with a rubber spatula so they don't burn. When the chips are just melted, add the soy or reduced-fat milk, one tablespoon at a time, and stir until smooth.

 You may need to add more soy or reduced-fat milk if the sauce is too thick. *NOTE: Reduced-fat milk will take longer to incorporate into the chocolate than the soy milk. Stir swiftly or use a wire whisk.*

SCORE A PERFECT TEN

Yes, a salon mani/pedi is a sweet treat, but you can *so* get amazing tips on your own. Follow these instructions and your mani will last a solid week and your pedi will stay put for two. Give yourself an hour or more to really let it all dry, which is majorly important for avoiding digit disasters like chips and smudges. Ready? Get painting…

FOR YOUR NAILS

1. Blast away old polish with a non-acetone remover. Then shape nails into rounded squares using a file.

2. Fill a bowl with warm water and add a bit of your fave bubble bath. Rinse off after a few minutes, and use a cotton-wrapped orange-wood stick to push back cuticles. Pop on lotion, let it sink in and relax.

3. Use a washcloth to remove leftover oils from your nails. Start with base coat to avoid chips. Swipe on two thin coats of polish, letting each dry. Apply a top coat, and you're done. In a rush? Dry for 10 minutes, then run hands under icy water to set. Voilà.

FOR YOUR TOES

1. Use a clipper to snip toenails straight across. Use a file to round off edges.

2. Let your tootsies splash around in warm water and soak for five minutes and then pat 'em dry.

3. Use a foot file to gently nix tough skin. Rinse!

4. A thick layer of lotion is a must. Let it sink in and then use a damp washcloth to wipe oils off the nails.

5. Like with your fingers, apply base coat, two coats of color and a top coat. Remember to wear sandals so you don't undo your work.

TOP SECRET

CONFIDEN

KEEP A **SECRET** LONGER

Promise you won't tell anyone? Keeping a secret can be like holding a sneeze in a pepper factory—but it doesn't have to be. If you've crossed your heart but can't keep it in, write about it in your journal. Too private even for your diary? Write it on a tiny piece of paper, rip it up and flush it down the toilet.

If telling the secret will crush the person who trusted you, wear a reminder on your wrist. Pull a bracelet onto your dominant hand (aka the one you write with) so you won't slip up. But remember: There are a couple secrets that even the best of friends should share with a trusted adult. If a friend confides she's hurting herself, being abused or otherwise in serious trouble, telling the right person (guidance counselor, clergy person, your mom) is a way to get her the help she needs. Trust us, she'll appreciate it in the long run.

8

ACE THE PSAT OR ANY OTHER TEST

9

Sitting down to a test and going blank stinks, especially when it comes to make-it-or-break-it exams. We asked the experts at the Sylvan Learning Center to weigh in on how to see sky-high scores. First, get super organized, whether with an old-fashioned planner or techy calendar app. Write down all of your big test days and assignments as soon as you know them. And then? It's time to get cracking. Girls who land the loftiest grades don't do so under some kind of magic spell. Nope, they do it by working diligently the entire time. For big standardized tests, you better believe they're studying over the summer, too.

To make preparation easier, make a point to really pay attention during class (duh, but seriously, it makes such a difference) and take neat, detailed notes. Doctors might famously have bad handwriting, but chicken scratch isn't the way to the A—messy notes will slow ya down. Psst: Ask the class brain if she'll let you take a peek at hers so you'll know how it's done. When you get home, take 20 minutes every day to read over your notes and highlight the most important stuff. If you keep up with what's going on, late nights spent cramming will be a thing of the past. If something is tripping you up, ask a teacher, parent or tutor for help ASAP.

LOVE IT!

On test day, wake up early and have a solid breakfast. When you start the exam, keep up the deep breaths. Make sure you go back and check your answers to ensure you filled in those pesky bubbles correctly and didn't skip anything. Exhale, and know you did your best, babe.

The night before the big exam, you should only need about an hour to go over the important things you've already learned. Remember to ease anxiety by getting your stuff ready the night before, eating breakfast that day and taking deep breaths all along the way. Oh yeah, and don't forget to sleep. Have a few extra minutes in the morning? Quickly go over your notes again to remind yourself that, "Hey, I know this!"

Simplifying Fractions

Name:

Change the fractions into lowest terms.

Well Done! (A+)

1) $\frac{28}{35} = $ 4/5 ✓   2) $\frac{32}{48} = $ 2/3 ✓   3) $\frac{6}{9} = $ 2/3 ✓

4) $\frac{2}{4} = $ 1/2 ✓   5) $\frac{18}{36} = $ 1/2 ✓   6) $\frac{21}{42} = $ 1/2 ✓

7) $\frac{2}{8} = $ 1/4 ✓   8) $\frac{24}{32} = $ 3/4 ✓   9) $\frac{10}{50} = $ 1/5 ✓

$\frac{10}{60} = $ 1/6 ✓   11) $\frac{6}{15} = $ 2/5 ✓   12) $\frac{8}{24} = $ 1/3 ✓

$\frac{6}{10} = $ 3/5 ✓   14) $\frac{20}{60} = $ 1/3 ✓   15) $\frac{45}{54} = $ 5/6

WRITE A **BETTER** ESSAY

Lots of girls get a case of the dread-o-ramas when a teacher assigns an essay, but these wordfests don't have to feel impossible—or even like a drag. Master this academic must, and you'll secretly dominate tons of subjects (from English to Social Studies) and be totally prepped for high school and college. Here's how to rock the doc...

1. READ. THOSE. DIRECTIONS. You might write a killer five pager on symbolism in *To Kill a Mockingbird*, but if your teacher wants a persuasive essay arguing for or against Boo Radley, well, you're not following directions. And that can kill your final grade, no matter how great your writing is.

2. BECOME BESTIES WITH THE THESIS STATEMENT. You might think your topic is oh-so-obvious (uh, it was assigned to you), but your teacher wants to know you can concisely make your point. So lay down that thesis statement—in middle school and high school, it's one sentence that encompasses the heart of your paper—and build around it. Three supporting ideas are often enough but, like we said, follow what your teacher doled out.

3. PLAN, PLAN, PLAN. Maybe you're an outliner or perhaps you like to jot ideas on notecards. Whatever it is, trust us that gold isn't just gonna flow out when you sit down at the keyboard. A little effort ahead of time will eliminate writer's block.*

4. PROOF IT. So, you've finished it! Hurrah! Not so fast. Make sure your

paper is complete at least 24 hours before your final deadline, no matter what. What looked perfect at 10 p.m. last night is likely to have errors in the morning. Get a good night's sleep, print it out and read it through. Then go back and make those changes.

11

GET EVERYWHERE
10 MINUTES EARLIER

Everyone knows being late is the worst, but it's easy to fall into the tardy trap. We asked a flight attendant for some advice, because airlines are strict about their schedules. "Showing up late says to everyone that you don't care about or respect them," says Marie Harville, who flies for American Airlines. Get this genius tip: "I plan when I need to leave the house, not when I have to be at work. Also, you never know what's going to happen between point A and point B, so allow a few extra minutes. Getting somewhere early is way better than rushing around and arriving to angry faces." So smart! Start planning your day as if the plane (err, bus) is going to take off without you, and you'll soon be soaring in with minutes to spare.

READ MORE BOOKS

Reading happens to be one of life's greatest—and cheapest—pleasures. It can open your mind, change your life's path and transport you to another time and place. Amazing. But with school, extracurrics and the constant buzz of life, many girls let reading for fun fall to the wayside—but wish they hadn't. Luckily, we have a no-fail plan for getting your nose back in the pages.

1 **Always carry a novel with you.** We asked for advice from someone who reads more books than most people—a college literature major. "Even if it's for only a few minutes, like in line at lunch or on the bus, I get a lot of reading done," says Belinda, who reads at least two novels a week (!) at the University of Oklahoma. A couple minutes here and there add up.

2 **Become BFFs with your librarian.** There are approximately 100 zillion books out there, so how's a girl to choose? Dust off your library card and write down a few titles you absolutely loved. Then head over to the library and chat up the person behind the desk. She likely has a bunch of suggestions, based on exactly what you heart. Keep an open mind, and always take a few books out at each visit to ensure you will end up with something you love.

3 **Only read what you like.** For school, you must finish what your teachers assign—that's a given. But outside the hallowed halls, why stick with a book you hate? Girls often feel like they "have" to finish a for-fun book, but then they get stuck in a reading never-never land. They're never reading the book they're working on, but never reading anything else either. They're just treading literary water. If you've read three or four chapters of a book but still don't like the story, the characters or the writing style, we give you permission to put it down. (Hint: this is why borrowing is so important...otherwise you might go broke.)

4 **Become a lit chick.** Starting or joining a book club is an amazing way to stay on track when it comes to page-turners. Either band together your BFFs or seek out people with similar tastes to your own by hanging posters at school or in the library or the local bookstore (calling all sci-fi geeks!). Before you know it, you'll be ticking off a novel a month, which is pretty impressive. If that's too much, aim for one every other month.

BE THE CLASS FAVORITE...
WITHOUT BEING A BROWN-NOSER

13

It's hard not to roll your eyes at the girl who brings Teach a shiny apple and offers to refill her coffee mug for the millionth time. But you don't have to be annoying to make a good impression. "Most of us teachers feel unimportant to our students," says Jan Hargrave, a body language expert and former high school teacher. "Your instructors are just people. If they get the feeling you like and respect them, they'll think fondly of you." Teachers heart when a kid listens in class, so pay attention and nod every so often. Lean forward a bit to emphasize that you're tuned in. And be sincere while you're listening—teachers can always smell a fake. Next, make eye contact and ask her questions to show you're involved. Oh, and smiling is key, too.

LOVE IT!

Aspiring to be the star? Spout off correct answers to your teacher's in-class questions. "So few kids are ready to go on with the day's lesson," says Jan. "Girls who have read the assignment will always stand out in their teacher's mind."

KEEP A GRATITUDE JASURNAL

14

Writing down what you're grateful for is a scientifically proven way (who knew?) to feel amazing about all that you're blessed with in your life. So snag a cute notebook from the dollar store or decorate a plain old one with a collage of words that inspire you. Keep it on your nightstand, and every couple of nights before you go to bed pen three things that you were grateful for that day. It's tempting to do it nightly, but the uplifting effect actually wears off if you go overboard. On Sunday evening, look back at everything you wrote down in the previous week and feel the good vibes wash over you.

LOVE IT!

Having trouble sticking with your journal? Create a reminder on your calendar or write it into your planner.

my diary

15 DECORATE YOUR ROOM WAY COOLER... FOR NO MONEY

IT HAPPENS TO THE BEST OF US: One minute our rooms seem super cute, and the next they're a shrine to everything we loved in first grade. Yikes. Making your room look more like y-o-u starts by packing away the toys you don't play with anymore. If you hate to see it all go, create a few shadowboxes to display different collections or blue ribbons. Then hang snapshots of you and friends in the frame of a dresser mirror, on the nightstand or in collage frames on the walls. And don't overlook yard sales. Sure, that wooden dresser is ugly now, but just about anything looks great after a few quick coats of white paint (and we bet you can find a gallon in the garage). Pick some wildflowers from the backyard, plunk them in a vase on your nightstand and kick back to admire your awesome new spot.

LOVE IT!

WE ADMIT IT: We can be total softies when it comes to beloved stuffed animals and T-shirts. If you can't part with a of your plushies, consider keeping one on your bed or bureau. And those worn-out fave tees? Ask Mom and Dad i you can have 'em stitched into a commemorative quilt.

BE THE BLOCK'S FAVORITE BABYSITTER

16

We found one universal rule when it comes to successful babysitting: Play with the kids! "Some girls see babysitting as a night of TV and talking on the phone to their friends," says Laura, a 10-year-old from New York who plans to start babysitting next year. "If a sitter ignores me, I tell my mom not to call her again. A babysitter should care about what the kids are doing." No callback equals no more babysitting money. Think about it.

ACTUALLY DRINK MORE WATER

17

Sipping H_2O has countless benefits, from stopping you from snacking so much (water makes you feel fuller) to putting the kibosh on headaches, but nearly everyone doesn't gulp enough. The solution? Always keep a BPA-free water bottle handy, and slip a few hair elastics or rubber bands around it (aim for 6–8 cups per day, so the number of bands will vary, based on your container). Every time you drink an entire bottle, take one off. At the end of the day, you should have zero bands.

LOVE IT!

Make your water taste even better by infusing it with tasty fruits and herbs. We love strawberry and cucumber or mint and lime or grapefruit. So good.

GIVE A GREAT GIFT

The best prezzie-presenters are the ones who pay attention. Make a note if your mom mentions she would love to grow veggies, and present her with a packet of seeds and a book on the topic at the next opportunity. Even if it's six months later, she'll totally appreciate that you were thinking of her. Missed that op? Think about something you think the person might want but wouldn't splurge on (remember: this is about her, not you!). Activity gifts are always awesome, too, like a day doing something you both totally love—together. Gift cards are OK, but add a personal touch by saying something like, "I know you've been dying for a new bag, and [this store] had so many cute ones, I thought you'd have a blast picking one out yourself!" Writing a great card seals in the sweetness.

LOVE IT!

One particularly good gift-giver in our lives actually keeps a running list of potential presents for all of her VIPs—parents, siblings, friends, etc. Some are big and some are small, but come Christmas and birthdays, there's no last-minute fretting over what exactly to dole out…it's all right there.

Memo No.
Date

☐ Mom

☐ Dad

☐ Sam

☐ April

HANDLE A STRESSFUL WEEK

19

Staring down a doozy? It's time to get organized, blocking out day-by-day and hour-by-hour accounts of your to-do's, including when you'll have downtime. Be honest with how long it will take for each activity: There's no way you can write a six-page history paper in an hour, so give yourself a reasonable chunk of time.

Then build in a little relaxation time every day. Now's not the moment to plot a Netflix marathon, but cut yourself some slack for at least an hour each night. We think some screen-free time is best. And remember: When things get hectic, sticking to your healthy-girl ways (exercising, good-for-you snacks, etc.) is even more critical. Running around on junk food and zero sleep will lead to a crash faster than you can say, "But I'm too busy for this!" Treat your bod well and your energy will soar, even if your sched is more scrambled than your dad's famous eggs.

Dashing out the door sans food may not seem like a big deal, but it's a recipe for scholastic disaster. Your bod needs brain food, and that comes in the form of your first meal. To ensure you always at least nosh some cereal, set your alarm 15 minutes earlier than you do now. (In a few days, your body will adapt, but going to bed a little earlier never hurt anyone.)

REMEMBER ANYTHING

Your keys, homework, wallet, concert tickets, lip gloss— just a few of the things on your Most Likely to Get Lost list. If only you could super charge your memory, you wouldn't waste another second pulling your room apart looking for your stuff.

Whenever you can't find or remember something, it's because you weren't aware of it in the first place, says Cynthia Green, Ph.D., founding director of the Memory Enhancement Program in New York. Put simply, you are doing things absentmindedly and your crazy sched doesn't help. **TRY THIS**: Next time you lay down your keys, be aware of your action, then imagine the key crashing to the ground. Add a surprising visual to every-thing you do—from putting away items to memorizing facts—and you'll be twice as likely to recall stuff later. Another memory jogger is, well, jogging. Studies show exercise pumps blood to your brain and boosts memory. So the next time you're racking your brain in search of something, take a walk or ride your bike. Sweating it off may be the best advice yet.

LOVE IT!

If you're super nervous about talking to your crush, spend som extra time hanging with your gu friends (or your bro's or BFF's). Remembering that guys are not s different from us (sorta) will hel you keep it real when you finally crack into that convo. Have a couple ideas of what to say, and then let the rest flow.

TALK TO ANY GUY

You'd think you were talking to Harry Styles the way your palms sweat and your eyes glue to the floor every time you're face-to-face with a guy. Lots of girls get antsy when guys are in the vicinity. You *can* overcome this.

If you're not used to boys, you could be clueless as to what to chat about. Maybe your heart is racing due to first-crush jitters. The excitement can wreak havoc on your composure. Just remember—even if the guy's a superstar, he's human, too. He probably feels just as awkward as you do. Get over the fear by taking baby steps. "First, start a simple conversation," suggests Chérie Carter-Scott, Ph.D., author of *If High School Is a Game, Here's How to Break the Rules*. "Say, 'I forgot my pen. Do you have one I can borrow?'" Ask him about a quiz or maybe sports, and then, slowly but surely, you'll graduate to longer conversations. If you're still shaky, there's always safety in numbers. "It's easier to be yourself with your girlfriends nearby," Chérie explains. "So interact with guys at a party or school sports event, when your friends are around. You'll have a bud right there to talk to if you need a break from the boys." And don't forget to just be yourself—you can never go wrong with that.

23

SAVE MORE CASH THIS WEEK

Lots of girls put off starting new habits until, well, never. Think "Next week I'll eat better" or "I'll start saving my allowance after Christmas" or whatever. But to start saving cash right this second, all you have to do is write down everything you spend. Trust us, if you had to log that $2.99 on hair ties and $5.99 on mascara into a notebook, would you really shell out for them…or would you suddenly remember that you own the same-ish thing at home already? Thinking before you buy and then committing to penning each purchase will put more coin in your purse—pronto.

BE LESS AFRAID

24

When you're really afraid of something and don't know why, it's called a phobia. Whether you're bug-phobic or homework-phobic (ha, ha), you *can* help yourself. First, make a mantra (a sentence you say in your head over and over again) that you can repeat to yourself when you're feeling scared: "There is nobody under my bed!" or "I could crush that ugly bug!" Mentally repeating something won't make your fears vanish, but it'll calm you and remind you that you're in charge of your thoughts. Then show that bug who's boss.

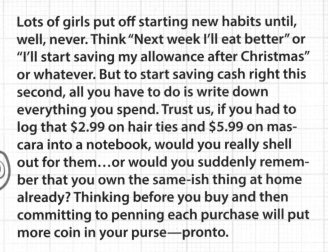

HAVE MORE GUY FRIENDS

To become one of the guys, treat the Y-chromosomes like you treat your girl buds—be nice, hang out, have fun...and make cool car and explosion noises whenever appropriate. If lack of exposure is the problem, get parental approval to throw a party with some friends and plan stuff that boys like as much as girls, such as a big game of soccer or an outing to zoom around in some go-karts. Parents don't approve of boy-girl bashes? Join a youth group or a coed club or band at school, and watch the friendships with boys appear. Whatever you do, don't talk about whether or not you should get bangs or who likes who at school. Just a hint.

25

LOVE LIFE UNPLUGGED

26

Being constantly connected can be majorly distracting, add to your anxiety and make easy tasks take twice as long (hello, homework). Creating a couple of tech-free times every day will help you remember just how great the world is, even without your cell or computer. Start by unplugging an hour before bed and giving yourself 20 gadget-free minutes in the a.m. This will allow you to unwind, sleep better and then start the day in a refreshing way. Write, stretch, pray—whatever will make you feel less stressed. Remember: Keeping track of how being unplugged makes you feel will encourage you to keep up the habit.

Then, add a couple more 30- to 50-minute chunks throughout the day, like when you're at dinner or doing homework. It'll feel awkward at first, but soon you'll appreciate how free and fab your mind feels without the urge to check for new pings. And don't panic: Your friends will get used to your new text-less sched—and we bet some will adopt it, too.

27 TRIUMPH AT TRYOUTS

What do you need to make the cut? "It takes effort, effort, effort to make any team," explains Majid Ali, a trainer in Los Angeles. "Whether you aspire to be a cheerleader or debate team queen, practicing like crazy can work like magic."

But there's more to it than that. The truth is that you don't have to be the absolute best to make the team. Coaches are always looking for desire, enthusiasm and potential, in addition to talent. One high school swim coach admits his favorite team member is pretty meh at freestyle, butterfly and backstroke. "But she's got the best attitude, which is vital to our team spirit," he says.

And on the big day? "Right before tryouts, breathe deeply and relax," Majid suggests. "Imagine yourself doing well. See yourself getting congratulated by your coach and friends."

You're golden, girl.

FIT IN WITH A NEW
GROUP OF **FRIENDS**

Whether you're the new girl or just expanding your friendship circle, it can be hard to mesh with a new crew. But making new buds is all about tuning in and being your sweet self. To know if you're vibing, look for key signs, like smiling, eye contact and people interested in what you're saying. Look for friends who make you feel comfortable and confident. They shouldn't put you down (even if they say "j/k!"), and you should enjoy your time with them, too.

Four rules to make friends if you're the newbie

1. BE POSITIVE: Remind yourself that things will get less awkward with time and give yourself major props for putting yourself out there.

2. BE YOURSELF: While it's great to start anew, never lie or exaggerate about your life or interests. People will see through your fibs.

3. BE INTERESTED: Pay attention to your new pals—notice their cool earrings, remember to say good luck on that big bio test, ask them about their weekends.

4. BE NICE: Try to avoid gossiping. You never know who used to be BFFs with whom or who may be offended by what you say. And remember: the so-called cool girls aren't the only ones worth buddying up with.

GET YOUR ENERGY
BACK AFTER SCHOOL

Raise your hand if your post-school routine looks something like this: Fling open the door, grab a snack and then make a beeline for the couch. Time to get that post-class energy back so you can pursue fun time with friends or at least finish your homework before dinner. To jolt yourself back to life after classes, have a big glass of water as soon as you get home. Then assess what your afternoon will look like (Big project? Ballet? Basketball?) and figure out if you should have a healthy snack to fuel yourself for later or go for a walk around the block to get the blood flowing. Do that daily, and we bet the couch will lose its appeal. Still no? Sign up for something that meets right after school so you have to get into a good groove after the bell.

30

DECORATE YOUR **LOCKER**

The cutest lockers are the ones that are a blend of the practical, the adorable and the personal. So each should be stashed with a cosmetic bag of must-haves: deodorant, toothbrush, pads or tampons, lip balm, hair ties, a brush, etc. Then figure out what works best for your school supplies: Should notebooks be up top or on the bottom? Where will you stash spare pens, pencils, erasers? Creating a theme or color scheme among your supplies will give it a so-you feel. Then use putty to paste up your schedule, pictures of your BFFs and a mini vision board for the year. We also recommend adding one sort of school spirit-y item, just for kicks, whether it's a snap of your soccer team or the pennant of your dream college. Classic!

PICK A SIGNATURE SCENT

There's something glam about having a perfume you rock on the daily. But where's a girl to begin? Narrow down which scent family you heart the most. Love all things clean and bright? Try citrus. Love the smell of crunching leaves? You're woodsy. Dig the scent of apple cider and cinnamon? Try oriental notes. Florals are an easy (and obvious!) pick for lots of girls.

To eliminate some of the choices, head to Sephora or a department store. Start by picking out several scents, spritz 'em onto blotting cards and take a whiff to test. Narrow it down to two faves and spritz each wrist. Stroll around the mall for 10 minutes to allow the scent to blend with your body chemistry. Pick your favorite out of the two, then ask for a sample. Test 'em out for a week, and then buy one or repeat.

BUY SHOES THAT ACTUALLY FIT

To snag kicks that don't cause mega pain or blisters, you gotta shoe shop in the afternoon. Being on your tootsies all day makes them swell a bit, which means if you go first thing in the a.m., your shoes won't feel fab when you pull 'em on at 7 p.m. to go out with your girls. We heart shopping online, but unless the place has free shipping and free returns, skip it in favor of a local shop (that you hit up after school). That way, you won't try on the most outta-this-world strappy sandals only to find out they don't actually fit your feet. Oh, and never, ever buy shoes that are too small, even if you LOVE them, they're on mega sale or you think they don't hurt that badly. You (and your tootsies) will just be miserable. Trust us, we've learned the hard way.

32

LOVE IT!

We know it can be tempting to go into the local shoe shop, find the size you want and then head online to find a cheaper pair. It's rude to make the salesperson do all the work and get none of the benefits. Instead, do your price research ahead of time, checking out sites like shopstyle.com to see who has the best prices before clicking.

SERVE A SHOWSTOPPING
ICE CREAM SUNDAE

It's just a fact of life: Everyone loves a couple scoops buried under some whipped cream. And sundaes happen to be a fun—and slightly fancy—dessert to make for your BFFs or your family. To make 'em extra chic, start with a pretty glass or bowl. Then use an ice cream scoop to dole out two perfect spheres. Add your fave sauce, whether that's salted caramel or classic chocolate. Next, sprinkle on a topping or two (we know it's tempting to add, like, six, but showing a little restraint keeps it classy). Break out the whipped cream, point the nozzle down and quickly turn your wrist two and a half times, to create a pretty white spire. Adorn your creation with nuts or sprinkles, and then add a cherry.

LOVE IT!

Homemade whipped cream is unbelievable—and easy to make. For starters, chill a metal mixing bowl in the fridge. When it's dessert time, add a cup of heavy cream and a teaspoon each of vanilla and sugar. Using a stand mixer set on medium, mix until it's fluffy (about 3 to 5 minutes). Done!

BOUNCE BACK
AFTER A BAD WEEK

Just because you came home totally deflated on Friday afternoon doesn't mean you have to slide right into a so-so or utterly sad weekend. Instead, write down five good things about the week. It can be as small as remembering that yesterday's lunch rocked or that you finally remembered to return that book to the library. Whatever it is, take a minute to acknowledge your blessings.

And that night? Don't feel pressure to make mega plans. Instead, try to think what might make ya smile. Maybe it's settling in for a funny flick with your BFF or even just enjoying a cheer-you-up dinner of spaghetti and meatballs with your parents. Remember: Mistakes are something to learn from, not dwell on, and freaking out if you said the wrong thing or made someone mad will just zap your energy and wear down your confidence. Hit the sack before the clock strikes Saturday so you can get plenty of zzz's, which often makes a bad week seems less terrible. A hot shower helps, too.

34

CURE SATURDAY BOREDOM

Once you're bored, it's almost impossible to think of exciting stuff to keep you busy. So figure out what to do with yourself *before* you become bored out of your gourd. There's always stuff you wish you could do if it weren't for your six tests/two papers/five parties/second cousin's wedding/whatever. Start a to-do list at those super busy times, and tuck that list away in a desk drawer or post it on your bulletin board. You'll have it handy next time a boring Saturday rolls around. Hey, it sure beats endless reruns.

Here are a few places to start, in case the boredom has already hit: Try a new recipe, go for a run, make a new playlist for your BFF, create your own stationery using stamps, write a story, call a faraway relative or your grandparents, draw something, jot down that volunteering idea you had, organize your camera phone pictures into a collage or go to the library and take out a new book.

WRIGGLE OUT OF
EMBARRASSMENT

Blam! There go your chili-cheese nachos—all over the cashier in the lunch line. Everyone is snickering, and all you want to do is crawl into the guacamole vat and die. You could either slither away into goofball obscurity...or you could make the most of your mishap. Lynn, a successful touring comedian, says humor is the cure for almost any embarrassing situation. If you trip, the worst thing you can do is pretend it never happened. Instead, act like you just finished a gold-grabbing gymnastics routine. Put your arms in the air and say, "That deserves a 10!" Then be sure to apologize to whomever you might have mangled, offer to help mop up the mess and move on. Always own up to your goof and make light of it—that takes the pressure off you.

Same if you blurt something silly—own the mistake. Say, "Wait, did I say that? Let me rewind. I meant to say, [insert correct phrase here]." Keep talking, and your slip should slip people's minds. Actually, everyone will forget your blunders ASAP, no matter what they are. Why? Simple—we're all worried about our own mess-ups.

36

HAVE A GREAT HAIR DAY EVERY DAY

For gorgeous hair, keep it squeaky clean and get trims about once every eight weeks. For problem hair that's frizzy or tangle prone, pro stylists recommend using leave-in conditioner—just comb a bit into damp hair and then let it air dry or blow it out. For a killer updo, pro Molly Ogden from Parlor Salon in New York recommends, "Always put your hair up while it's still a little damp so the hair is sort of glued to itself." Gotta dash out of the house, like, now? Try pulling your hair up and out of your face in a pretty topknot. Or twist up a quick 'n' easy side braid and sling it over your shoulder. Too cute.

You've been psyched for your BFF's coed bonfire for weeks. But your mom is more likely to buy you a pony than let you attend. You'd be surprised if she even stretches the curfew for you. Too bad you can't work mind magic on her. The truth is, it's nearly impossible to get mom to bend big rules for a one-off event. The better tack to take? Show your parents you're trustworthy and responsible on the regular. So keep your word (yes, even to clean your room, so your cousin can bunk up with you, ohh, tomorrow), do your chores and plug away on all your school assignments. While it might sound like a drag, displaying your more mature side on the daily (not just when you want something) will prove to your parents that you're not only growing up, but that you're able to make smart choices on your own.

38

After you've been on your best for a few months, ask your mom if you can chat. Remember to wait for a moment when she's not so stressed. Then present her with your proposition: maybe you'd like to extend your curfew by an hour, wear a li'l mascara with your lip gloss, attend the occasional boy-girl party. And then give her time to think about it. When it's all over, say thanks and drop it, regardless of her final decision. Throwing a fit weakens your future negotiating powers. And keep being helpful, OK?

CONVINCE MOM
TO BE A LI'L MORE LENIENT

39 GET ELECTED CLASS PRESIDENT

It doesn't matter who you're up against—you can sweep the school election. Honor students, homecoming queens and teachers' pets don't stand a chance if you follow our suggestions. First, be friendly and outgoing, for obvious reasons. "People who win have the right attitude—humble, not overconfident or too serious," says Jeff Marx, author of *How to Win a High School Election*. Winning candidates also talk to everyone who votes, not just their friends or the popular people. And you'd be surprised how many kids don't actually vote—reach out to them and convince them to cast one in your favor. "The person with the most support doesn't win, the person who gets the most *votes* does," Jeff says. Finally, just like a candidate for the White House, you need name recognition. So hang a few posters around school with your name in big, bold letters. And when it comes to the speech? "Nothing wins the attention of high school students like humor," Jeff say. Keeping it short 'n' sweet helps, too. But no matter what, stay true to yourself. None of these tips will work long term if you're faking it—not to mention you want to win for the right reasons. Get ready to rule the school, girlfriend.

MAKE THE WEEKEND LAST LONGER

40

o really revel in the 2.5
ays you have off each
eek, work on appreciat-
g every little moment.
stead of imagining your
aturday on Friday night,
njoy yourself right this
cond. Many of us con-
antly ponder (and fret
out!) the future, which
n zap the happiness
ut of the current instant.
nother hint? Seriously
eeping in isn't great for
ur bod, and it sucks up a
hole lotta time. Hop out of
ed early-ish on Saturday
nd Sunday a.m., and you'll
dd four or five hours to
ur weekend. Perfect.

LOVE IT!

Some girls heart a lazy weekend, but we love kickstarting a
Saturday with a tough workout,
like a Pilates class, a jog with
your BFF or some kung fu. Not
only will it allow you to brush off
any lingering bad feelings from
the school week, but it'll infuse
some happy, healthy-girl vibes
into the weekend.

SPEAK UP
IN ANY SITCH

Expressing yourself isn't just about what you say—it's about how you say it. It's hard for others to take you seriously if you're slouching, mumbling, chewing gum or fidgeting. So focus on oozing confidence with bold body language. Stand up straight, make direct eye contact and speak clearly. Set up a practice session with a bud, your grandmother or your mom. Have them come at you with the issue at hand ("Can you babysit for half the price?") then give your answer in a steady, even tone. Remember: Ending your statements with a question mark or higher pitch will show self-doubt (it's tough to hear this in yourself, so ask a friend). Brevity is key: Quick, to-the-point answers lessen the amount of time the other person has to talk you out of your mind-set. Soon, you'll be heard in no time.

41

ORDER **HEALTHY** AT A FAST FOOD JOINT

42

The occasional stop at a food court is inevitable (like with your band or on the way home from away games), but that doesn't mean you have to resign yourself to a gut-buster or yet another salad topped with chicken. First off, fast food salads are often swimming in dressing, croutons and cheese. So if you really want to eat clean on the fly, ask for dressing on the side and skip the other add-ons. Make sure your salad has a source of protein like beans, an egg or grilled meat. Want a sandwich? Bypass the fried patties, and go for a single burger or grilled chicken—no mayo, no cheese. Instead, top it with veggies or even hot sauce to spice things up. Snag water to drink and a healthy side, like apple slices. Can't live without fries? Order a small and split 'em with someone. And remember: Never super size!

HAVE FEWER FIGHTS WITH YOUR FRIENDS

T HAPPENS TO EVERYONE. One day everything's cool, the next day all your friends are ticked off at you and you don't even know why. How do you keep this from happening? Treat other people as you want to be treated. If you think you've irked a pal, tell her you're sorry and promise to be more careful of her feelings. If a friend does something to annoy you, tell her nicely why it gets under your skin…then forgive her. And let's just agree once and for all—the silent treatment is the worst thing to do, so never unleash it on anyone.

BUST A **BAD HABIT**

The first step to leaving your nail biting or over-liking behind ("I, like, would, like, love it!") is to acknowledge that you want to quit and commit to doing so. Then spend a couple of days keeping track of how often you unleash your trait, and write down how less-than-awesome you feel when it happens. Finally, find something you can do instead of the habit or a healthy way you'll sock it out of your system. If you bite your nails, for example, you could keep up with your manis to avoid gnawing. If you want to nix junk food, start drinking more water and stashing fruit in your backpack. If you say "like" or "um" too much, think before you speak and always talk slowly, so you enunciate each word and have time to compose your thoughts before blurting out whatever comes to mind. Don't forget to give yourself plenty of time to drop the trait, too. It can take months before you fully ditch the thing that's dragging you down. One day, you'll wake up and realize your bad habit has totally, like, vanished...and you'll never look back.

LOVE IT!

Asking for help when heaving an old habit is helpful. Just because it's yours doesn't mean you've got to deal with it alone. Let your buds and family know what you're up to and ask for their help as you kick your crutch.

FIGURE OUT WHAT MAKES
YOU HAPPY

45

Close your eyes for a sec, and think of three times you've been seriously happy lately (or even think back to when you were a little kid!). Don't judge yourself for what bubbles up; it could be something small, like when you were shooting hoops with Dad, or maybe it was just when you were day-dreaming and doodling in your room. Nothing comes to mind? Pay attention, and look for moments when you totally lose track of time because you're so enthralled with the task at hand (science says that's a telltale sign that you're enjoying what you're doing). Keep a list of your joy-makers, whether it's going for walks, getting all A's or heading to the beach. And then? Make time for those activities, and you'll be grinning in no time.

LOVE IT!

Some girls might find their list is filled with activities that are so amazing they can't do them on the regular (like trips to Disney or horseback riding). The thing is, when you're truly passionate about something, even learning about your happy place can bring a smile to your face. Get exploring, and you'll feel connected fast.

...AND WHAT YOU NEED TO SLOG THROUGH

We want your life to be chock-full of laughter and happiness—and so do you (duh!). But the truth is, there are often things we have to do that will make everything better in the long run. So even if algebra homework makes you cringe, well, you know where this is going...you have to power through! That said, figure out how to make those moments less painful. Maybe it's mapping out why it's so important (such as, if you want to go to college, you have to get great grades) and then how to improve your outlook. Getting a tutor might help. Otherwise try studying with a buddy or reward yourself each time you tackle one of your least-fave tasks. A bit of suffering now (and, really, the procrastination is often way worse) can help you reach long-term goals and make your future that much more amazing.

46

SAY SORRY...
BUT NOT TOO MUCH

I'm SORRY !!

47

One genuine apology is worth about a million squeals of "Soooooo sorrrrrry!" To work on making your *mea culpa* more heartfelt, take a second to collect your thoughts. Did you really mess up or hurt someone's feelings? If so, approach the person and tell them straight-up that you're sorry "x" happened. You didn't mean to cause them pain, and you hope the two of you can patch it over. Then listen to their response and shoot them a smile or a hug. Remember: Saying sorry for every little thing ("Can I have a glass of water...sorry!") makes people think you lack confidence, so only dish out the "s" word when it's really what you mean.

PEN AN AMAZING
THANK YOU NOTE

Thank you!

The best expressions of gratitude start with cute paper. Head to the stationery store or craft your own card. Then draft out what you're going to say on another sheet of paper: explain what you liked about the gift or exactly what you're thankful for. Keep the note short, sweet and specific. If someone passed along moolah, you don't have to call out the exact amount, but you could always mention that you're saving for college and every bit helps or that you'll use the gift on your upcoming class trip to a museum or whatever. Sending a thank-you every time someone gives you a gift is critical. People love knowing their prezzies were appreciated...and it's just plain polite.

FIND A CAUSE

Lending a hand is super important. Not only does it help lift up another person, place or puppy, it actually will boost your spirit and help remind you how blessed you are. But where to begin? Take a few minutes to ponder what you think is seriously unjust in the world. It could be hunger: Maybe you hate that some kids go to bed without a real dinner. Maybe you wish animals didn't have to suffer, or that kids didn't get cancer, or maybe it just makes you sad that the old playground you used to love has fallen into such disrepair. Some girls like to start with something close to their heart, like raising funds and running in road races that lead to medical research (especially if an aunt or grandparent had that illness).

Think hard until you come up with something that gets you fired up. Then do a couple of Google searches, talk to your parents or people in your hometown or make a phone call (or three) until you find a way to get involved with your cause. If it's something you care about and talk about, we know you'll find other people who are trying to make a difference, too. Every little bit helps!

GET A **HAIRCUT** YOU HEART

5O

When it comes to chopping your locks, saying "just a trim" or "I don't know" just doesn't, well, cut it. If you want to make your hair shiny, ask your stylist to show you exactly where she needs to snip in order to get rid of the dead ends. Then, give her the A-OK, knowing your hair will be healthier for it. Want a whole different style? Find a few celebrities with similar hair textures (like straight, wavy or curly) or face shapes with cuts you heart (we're keeping it plural, because often it takes more than one inspiration shot to find a style that you love and will look good on you). Show the pictures to your stylist and get her opinion before she brings the scissors anywhere near your mane.

NEVER GET HOMESICK AT CAMP AGAIN

Before you head off to sleepaway camp, pack a few pictures of your friends and fam and create a playlist of songs you love. When you have those missing-Mama moments, unearth your mementos and take a minute to cheer yourself up. Or write a letter home (so charmingly old school) and let them know all the fun things you've been doing. Remembering how you had a blast canoeing and roasting 'shmallows will lift your spirits.

But don't stay in your bunk pining away for other peeps and places. Get involved in as many activities as possible so you'll be having too much fun to feel sad. And confide in another camper—she might feel the same. Plus, opening up, being real and bonding is a way to score friends for the summer and for life. Who's homesick? Not you!

It's no secret that everyone and their toddler seems totally glued to their smartphone. But learning how to just be is super important, so start by avoiding looking at the screen the next time you're solo…and feeling a little awkward. Instead, make a point to take in the world around you, noting the little things like the baker across the street who is putting some seriously tasty-looking sticky buns in the window, or the cute boy across the aisle on the field trip bus. Observing—and being engaged—with the world around you unlocks your imagination. Plus stashing your iWhat-ever in your purse helps keep that go-go-go stress at bay. The next time you're just chillin' and reach for your pocket? Don't. Take a deep breath, look around and take in the moment: You'll never be in this time and place again.

BE ALONE WITHOUT JUST GLAZING OUT ON YOUR PHONE

BUST A BREAKOUT

The moment you feel a pimple popping up, start living by the two Ps: No picking and no panicking. Instead, make sure you're drinking plenty of water and eating tons of veggies—good nutrition helps your body heal. As for the spot itself? Avoid exfoliating, and use a spot treatment to nix inflammation and redness. If it's really bugging you, dab on a tiny bit of concealer so you can't see it. Then pull your hair off your face and get ready to head out into the world. It might seem like a monster, but everyone else has their own stuff going on, so they won't even notice. Trust.

OUR NO-FAIL SKIN ROUTINE

1. **Wash your face every night, and apply a light moisturizer.**

2. **Every a.m., wash, treat any zits and apply sunscreen.**

3. **Once a week, use a gentle exfoliator to buff away dead skin.**

4. **If this doesn't keep your skin mostly fab (occasional breakouts are totally normal during your teen years), consult a derm about how to deal with your acne. She'll be able to tailor a treatment to your skin.**

DO A SPLIT

54

Guess what? You don't have to be a ballerina, yogi or dancer to secretly be a bendy babe. If you are committed, you can do a split within a couple of months. Each night after your shower, spend 15 minutes stretching, focusing on your hamstrings. Here's a fave: start standing on your knees, with your knees at hip width. Stick one leg out straight in front of you, with your toes pointing up. Slowly, lean over that lead leg, with your hands on the floor, one on each side of your leg. Hold that for ten breaths, and then switch sides. After a week or so, start sliding into a split from there (even if you don't get low) and hold that for 5 to 10 breaths. Keep practicing, and you'll perfect it in no time.

MAKE SOMEONE'S DAY

Why not do something nice for a friend, family member or, hey, even a long-lost cousin's boyfriend's next-door neighbor? Spread a little love! Just think how great you feel when someone does something unexpectedly sweet for you. "Besides the obvious, going out of your way for someone else proves the world isn't such a competitive, tough place," explains Danny Seo, professional do-gooder and author of *Generation React*. "When we worry about grades, popularity and other everyday stuff, we forget that it's other people who really matter most to us." You don't have to throw someone a no-holds-barred birthday bash or buy your sis a pair of new boots to show you care. Instead, tell your friend she's a great listener or wash the dishes for your mom without being asked. Help an elderly lady with her grocery bags, or offer to babysit your neighbor's toddlers—for free. If you're having a lousy afternoon, this kind of stuff can work wonders for lifting a sour mood.

55

MAKE YOUR OWN
LIP BALM

Loaded with cranberries, our fave DIY lippie has a festive, holiday feel—perfect for gifting to all your girls. But the pretty, sheer hue is gorgeous all year long.

WHAT YOU'LL NEED:

• 1 tablespoon almond oil

• 10 fresh cranberries

• 1 teaspoon honey

• Microwave-safe bowl

• Spoon

• Fine sieve

• Tubes or pots for lip balm (find 'em at any craft store)

WHAT YOU'LL DO: Pour the almond oil, cranberries and honey into a bowl and microwave for short stints until it begins to boil (try 30 seconds at a time…and be careful!). Remove the bowl, grab your spoon and gently crush the cranberries. Stir the mixture well, then strain the liquid through a fine sieve to remove the bits of cranberry that remain. Pour the lip balm into your containers, and get ready to rock a pretty pout.

EMBRACE YOUR GEEKY SIDE

Lots of girls spend tons of time hiding from who they really are, shrugging off their so-called dorky habits. But guess what? The "weird" stuff you like is part of who you are—and might lead to a seriously cool internship or job in the future, or just a life-long hobby that makes you happy. Love to Photoshop every pic you take until you have the perfect Instagram? Tweak away. Obsessed with obscure French movies from the 1960s? Soak 'em up. Don't want to go it alone? Have friends join you or sign up for (or start!) a club that supports your passion. Spending a Saturday with like-minded comic book fans might just be what you need…and that's A-OK.

57

KNOW IF YOU SHOULD
BUY THAT PURSE

58

Retail regret is something we all hate, but how do you avoid it? Easy. Some chicas get into the habit of shopping to bust stress or boredom and wind up on buying sprees, shelling out their hard-earned cash for things they don't need. Others can't make up their mind about a potential purchase and buy stuff they aren't absolutely in love with. Not anymore. Ask yourself if you *really* need whatever shiny bauble you're coveting. Will you use it? Wear it? More than once? Imagine you didn't buy it…what would you use/wear/do instead? Consider all of these Qs before you get to the cash register. And as for the thing that's kinda-sorta out of your budget? If you'll use it a lot (jeans, everyday shoes, a new tote that'll take you from fall to spring), consider splurging. If it's something you won't use a ton or could find cheaper elsewhere—aka anything trendy or super seasonal—we say skip it. Now you're shopping smart.

ASK FOR HELP

As girls, we sometimes feel pressure to be able to do it all—be an awesome daughter, get great grades and excel at every activity on the planet. But sometimes the pressure can be too much…and you end up being pulled in a million different directions or feeling like things just aren't right. In those moments, it's time to call in the reinforcements. Whether you're struggling in a class or can't handle the stress, ask Mom, Dad, a fave teacher or the school counselor if you can talk when they have free time. Be straightforward: You're having trouble with "x" and would like their advice. Think about it as if you were helping your BFF: You'd want her to get the support she needs, and the same is true when it comes to you. And finally, pray about it!

TEACH YOURSELF
HOW TO FRENCH BRAID

Plaiting your own mane is totally doable…with a little practice. Start by taking a small section of hair from the front and break it into three smaller chunks. Take the left chunk and cross it in between the other two strands. Then take the right chunk and cross it into the middle. Now, as you take the chunk that is now on the left side, add a little bit more of the loose hair to the section, making it a li'l bit bigger. Again, cross it in between the other two sections. Then take the right section and add a little more hair to it, too. Cross it in between the other two sections.

Keep repeating this pattern until there is no more hair to add from each side (normally a little before when you reach the nape of your neck). From there, just normally braid your hair, securing it at the end with an elastic. Pretty, and not as tough as it looks, right?

LOVE IT!

Step up your braid game by going for a fishtail. Grab all of your hair into a ponytail at the nape of your neck. Divide into two sections. Take a small piece from the outside of the right section and cross it over to the left section. Do the same from the left side to the right. Repeat until you run out of hair, and secure with an elastic.

HAVE FUN ON A RAINY DAY

Here are our 10 favorite, mostly free ways to have a blast when the great outdoors is dishing out a full-on deluge…

1. GO GLAMPING—indoors. Use old tablecloths to set up a tent in the living room, and then roast marshmallows over a candle flame (make sure it's nontoxic) or bake some s'mores cookies. And then? Tell ghost stories while the rain rages.

2. RELIVE YOUR YOUTH. Why not have a throwback day, where you re-watch your fave Disney movie, reread your favorite kid's book (or six…) and make a snack you used to dig back in the day, like butterscotch pudding and Nilla wafers. So fun.

3. SHOW YOUR SKILLS. Gather your sibs or nearby buds and put on a talent show for each other. Celebrate all of your mad skills with a round of sundaes.

4. BECOME A YOUTUBE STAR. Create your own music videos for your favorite songs. Perform live for your parents, record on your cell or post it to a private YouTube link and then send it to faraway friends and relatives.

5. BAKE IT UP, BABE. Why not host a sweet cook-off, and give the outcome to an older neighbor or relative? We promise we won't tell if you keep a couple treats for your generous self.

6. TEE TIME. Snag a plain white tee, and go crazy (flip to number 86 for some serious inspiration).

7. GAME ON. Pull out the old Scrabble board and challenge yourself with a themed round. Harry Potter vs. Twilight words? You bet!

8. LEARN SOMETHING (ANYTHING). When you're straight-up stuck inside, it's an ideal time for giving yourself a little lesson in… whatever you're been meaning to learn. Open up some YouTube vids and start tap dancing.

9. MANI-CURED. Paint your way to a gorgeous hurricane manicure. Rain drops? Swirling wind? Caution tape? Go wild! (Or embrace your sunny side and the yellow polish and watch the rain, rain go away.)

10. COOL COLLAGE. Got a pile of old mags squirreled away? Snag a piece of poster board and get snipping. To make something a little more permanent, use some Mod Podge and revamp some of your picture frames with inspiring phrases. Too cute.

61

62 CLEAN YOUR CLOSET

OK, so unearthing all the junk from your walk-in isn't a walk in the park, but it'll make you feel refreshed and way less frazzled. Spend a Saturday afternoon pulling everything out of your space. Lump your clothes, shoes and gear into three piles: keep, donate, toss. Then neatly fold up all your off-season stuff and stash it into bins. Next, organize your clothing by color and hang it back in your closet. Bag up the other two piles and take care of them accordingly. And don't forget to vacuum up any rogue dust bunnies!

The next time you trot out of town, create a custom packing list on your computer, including everything you MIGHT need for your time away. Check the weather, and then pull clothes and accessories accordingly (if it's winter, pack ear muffs; if it's summer, don't forget the straw hat). Bring one outfit for each day you're there, plus a couple extra tops, pairs of socks and underwear.

Check in with your mom or whoever is planning the trip to see if there are any special activities, like a fancy brunch, or if your hotel has a pool. If you're going to be active, don't forget sneakers, even more socks and a sports bra. No matter what the forecast says, we think it's great to bring a light, snuggly sweater and a rain jacket, just in case. Think we're nuts? During the summer, some people like to crank the AC, and you never know when it's gonna sprinkle (or, worse, downpour).

Next, open up your suitcase, place your list on the flap and start checking off items as you pop them into your bag. Pack your toiletries in a resealable plastic bag and then tuck them into your cosmetic case. Don't forget extras, like glasses (if you wear 'em), contacts, sunnies, pads or tampons, contact solution, retainer, etc. You know that master packing list you just made? Save it, and add to it every time you jet. That way, you'll never forget a thing.

LOVE IT!

When we travel, we always bring one light dress, even if it seems like the trip is crazy casual. (Trust us, there will be a fun dinner, even if you're camping!) It's also easy if you pack mix 'n' matchables—aka a bunch of different pieces that go well together—instead of major prints. We travel light, but we like to have lots of options.

NEVER **GOSSIP** AGAIN

Gossiping is a slippery slope. It seems harmless, but the next thing you know, you're constantly gabbing about everyone under the sun. How to quit the noise? Every time you catch yourself opening your mouth to say something about someone, simply *don't*. Once you've stopped for about a month, it's easy to continue on your no-gab plan. It's like our BFF, who never, ever tried pecan pie—she thought if she started eating it, she'd become hooked on the sweet treat and it would trash her healthy-girl ways. Not gossiping is good for your soul, and by never doing it, you'll be less tempted to pass along what you heard about so-and-so.

MAKE A WHITE T-SHIRT AND JEANS LOOK CUTE

The secret to making denim and a tee seem stunning is the shoes and accessories. A few strands of long beads and boots (or strappy sandals) lends a boho vibe. Toss on your ballerina flats and a floaty scarf, and you've got that chic thing down. Slip into some moto boots and pop on a blazer, and you're indie cool. We could go on and on, but it's mostly about having fun with the rest of your getup and carrying yourself with an awesome attitude.

Shailene Woodley

65

BUCKLE DOWN
ON A TOUGH SUBJECT

When it comes to homework, most girls go right for the subject they like first. It seems like a no-brainer: Get the easy stuff out of the way and then tackle those toughies. Turns out, that zaps your energy and leaves you feeling even more drained as you attempt to plow through the subject that's stumping you. So approach your tough course with the Band-Aid method: Get it over with first and then move on to the less intense stuff. Started it, but super stuck? That's OK. Call a friend or a parent for help. They're not around? Move on to the next assignment and circle back when your phone-a-friend is available.

67

QUIT PROCRASTINATING

You meant to stop procrastinating, but…yeah, we get it. To nix the avoidance, schedule out your time better. Never want to do homework right after school? That's fine. Give yourself a half an hour to chill, but then start your work right at 4 p.m. Plotting out exactly when you'll work and when you'll rest gets rid of that wiggle room ("I'll do it later…"). Make an appointment with yourself, and stick to it. You're about to find a lot of free time.

POWER THROUGH YOUR **PERIOD**

Ugh, we get cramps just thinking about PMS. But your new visits from Aunt Flo don't have to be a nightmare. Even if your cycle leaves you listless, make a point to eat well, drink plenty of water and exercise, even if it's just a walk or a little light stretching. Your bod might be asking for brownies and bed time, but succumbing to every craving will make you feel worse every single time. We're not saying you have to attempt a triathlon during that time of the month, but stay active and positive and it'll get better. Remember: See a doc if the pain is too intense.

LOVE IT!

Our PMS kit includes: plenty of H₂0, vitamins, a hot water bottle, pumpkin seeds (the magnesium is good for nixing cramps) and dark chocolate. Don't go overboard on any of it, but occasionally pulling couch duty with your water bottle on your belly and a square of chocolate in your mouth will help. Just sayin'.

MAKE PEACE
WITH YOUR BOD

69

Small countries could be powered with the energy girls waste worrying about their bodies. Whether you wish your chest was bigger or smaller or your legs were longer or your stomach was flatter, well, just stop. Girls always want what they don't have, and everyone's body changes at different speeds. Instead of fretting, it's best to just attempt to make peace with what you've got. But how? Whenever you're feeling down, look in the mirror and find one specific thing you love about yourself—and say it out loud. Write Post-it notes and stick 'em around your room if you need encouragement. Remind yourself that God made you the way he did for a reason. But the biggest thing is to never compare yourself to other girls. As the saying goes, comparison is the thief of joy, and wishing you had what some other girl's got will never, ever make you feel better. So just don't, OK?

FORGIVE YOURSELF FOR THAT THING

70

If you and your BFF were in a fight, you'd hope you two could hash it out, forgive each other and move on without holding grudges, right? It's absolutely the same thing when it comes to you. So have a convo in your head, pray or write in your journal about whatever it is you did or said that you can't get over. Maybe you lied to your mom or failed a class or teased your little bro a lot when you were younger. Whatever it is, release it. You might have to remind yourself a few times, but soon you'll start to let go of the lingering bad feelings and patch things over with your soul. And just remember, if God can forgive you, you can forgive yourself.

PICK OUT SHAMPOO, MOISTURIZER, ETC. AT THE DRUGSTORE

To avoid endlessly wandering through the drugstore wondering what on earth to buy, figure out your skin and hair type. Is your hair fine, thick, curly, wavy, dry (aka, it breaks quickly), coarse or dandruff- or grease-prone? There are products to address each and every type and issue, so seek those out and then find a smell you heart. (Note: Dandruff shampoos tend to have a chemical odor...opt for the tea tree variety.)

When it comes to skin, it's the same deal. Got acne, dryness, combination (your cheeks are dry, but your nose and forehead get shiny) or oily skin? Snag a moisturizer and cleanser to treat those issues. Certain pharmacies, like CVS, allow you to return products if you have the receipt, so if you do choose the wrong one, bring it back. Also, always test out a product for a month before you make any decisions. Skin and hair take time to adjust to changes.

PACK AN AWESOME PICNIC

Simple (but secretly fancy!) food works best for an afternoon outdoor meal. To up your picnic game, start with a loaf of good bread, like a French baguette. Thick bread ensures your sammies won't get super soggy. Then start piling on your meats, cheeses or veggies. If you're adding slices of tomato, keep them in a separate container to avoid sogginess. Wrap sandwiches in plastic wrap, then stick them in big baggies. Toss sammies in a cooler or lunch bag, along with an ice pack wrapped in a tea towel. Now squirrel away some tasty sides, like apple slices or pretzels. Frozen grapes or homemade cookies also make yummy open-air desserts. Bring a couple bottles of water and fill one thermos with an Arnold Palmer—a mix of unsweetened iced tea and lemonade. To take it to the next level, pay attention to the details, like adding a pretty blanket to your bike basket and toting cloth napkins and real flatware. Don't forget a good book!

LOVE IT!

Elevate your picnic even more by creating a cute and colorful theme. If you heart red, go for tomato and mozzarella sandwiches (remember: add the tomato when you arrive!), with a side of red skin potato salad and watermelon for dessert. To sip? Raspberry lemonade, of course. So pretty.

72

LEAVE A GREAT NOTE IN SOMEONE'S YEARBOOK

You don't have to be voted Most Popular to leave the best missive in the back of someone's book. To make it sweet, let the person know how much you appreciate their friendship ("So happy we got closer this year!") or share a memory ("It was a blast spending the day at Canobie Lake!") or something you love about the person ("You're the best teammate!"). Then write another line that wraps up the year or includes an inside joke from the past few months, like how much you'll miss sitting near her in Bio or how you'll never forget when your lip synch group nailed the victory. End it with a sentence about how you hope you two hang out over the summer or that you hope she has fun at camp or how you're psyched to be on JV together next year. That's it! Heart, you.

73

TRUST
YOUR GUT

s that your conscience...or the ham sandwich you had for lunch? Learning how to trust your gut is easier than it seems. The next time you're in a sticky situation, pay attention. We bet there's some kind of rumbling in your tummy. Tune in every time your inner voice is saying "this is awesome" or "this is really wrong." (Some girls have a combo gut and voice, some girls have more of a tugging in their heart, so you have to figure out what *your* signal is.) If you get the feeling you're in a place that's unsafe or you're about to do something you shouldn't...well, you're probably right. It'll take a bit to really hone the skill, but soon you'll be listening to your gut all the time.

TELL A JOKE

Your humorous side is like a muscle—the more you use it, the stronger it gets. The best way to score some laughs? Just wait for a pause in conversation that works as a prompt to your joke. Say, "That reminds me of a story I heard," and then launch right into it. Don't ever force a joke, because then there's extra pressure for it to be funny. And have no fear if you fumble through it—your mistakes will add to the humor. Just make sure you follow the golden rule: Don't start a joke unless you do, in fact, remember the punch line. If all else fails? Go with the classics: "Knock, knock." "Who's there?" "Interrupting cow." When your pals are in the middle of replying, "Interrupting cow who?" interrupt them and say, "Moo!" Heh. Still need practice? Hang around funny people, and borrow a few of their best lines.

BE THE STAR OF THE PARTY

76

No need to be a shy violet at the next bash—it's easier than you think to tap into your inner party princess. First, make a confident entrance. Arrive fashionably late (that's about 30 minutes), so you can be sure your friends are already there (you'll feel much more at ease if you know your crew will rush over to you to say "hi" when you arrive). Next, add an eye-catching element to your outfit. A bold-colored top, glittery cardi or even a just-for-fun accessory like a boa will draw all eyes to you. Whatever you choose, make it a piece you love—you want your clothes to be an extension of you. And it never hurts to have a gimmick: Download the latest photo enhancement app on your phone so everyone can instantly add funny doodles to their party pics. Last, but not least, be a wonderful conversationalist. Who doesn't want to talk to the girl who says "hi" and smiles at everyone (be friendly!), asks questions (instead of talking nonstop) and tells jokes (see #75). The bottom line? Have fun…and be yourself.

SUMMER SALE!

20

YOUR HIGHES
PRICED ITEM

Save

GET GOOD DEALS AT THE MALL

77

There's no reason to help huge, bajillionaire companies fatten up their bank accounts. Instead, plump up your own by saving beaucoup bucks on everything you buy. Our shopping motto? Never pay full price! All stores—from Target to fancy ones like Neiman Marcus—mark down goodies to make room for the new merchandise that constantly arrives. If you're serious about saving, stick to the sale racks. Be patient, as most full-price clothes usually wind up being discounted within a month. But, the rule of the sale rack isn't always true at discount outlets, where stores do heavy markdowns on damaged duds or stuff that just won't sell. So while you can get some good deals at these special stores, be extra careful. Watch for stains, pulls and mislabeled sizes. Have a fave chain store? Most of them have a specific day devoted to price-slashing. Talk to a sales associate and ask her when those prices fall. And sign up for store newsletters: You'll get advance word on sales and the chance to score deals before everyone else. Finally, look online. Almost all mall retailers now have a sale page—and sites often have even better sale selections than stores do. Now you're smartly dressed!

Whether you just.can't.take. school stress anymore or your brother has irked you beyond belief, it is possible to calm yourself down after you've started to spiral. Whenever you feel the sure signs that you're gonna flip (maybe your temper has flared or your face is hot), take a time-out. It might seem like you have to handle the issue at hand right now or like it's impossible to stop yourself from exploding, but that's just not the case. Give yourself an entire minute— either in the bathroom or away from whomever you're with—to take deep breaths. Close your eyes and tell yourself, "I am calm." (Repeat if necessary.) After a few steady inhales and exhales and reminding yourself that you can handle whatever comes your way, you'll be ready to face the world with a fresh, new outlook—and with the potential tantrum in your past.

STOP A FREAKOUT
AFTER IT'S STARTED

78

RECONNECT
WITH AN OLD FRIEND

Some girls think that just because they haven't kept in touch with an old bud, the girl has become a former friend. But that's just not true! It's totally possible to link back up with a camp bunkmate or preschool pal—and we don't just mean on Facebook. To restart a real friendship, give your girl a call or write a note. Let her know you're sorry so much time has slipped by and that you'd love to hear all about her awesome life. Then pick a date to see if she can sleep over...and let her know you're open to other options, too. It might seem awkward for the first five seconds, but as soon as you two get gabbing, we bet it will be just like old times. Or maybe even better.

Hi! How've you been?

80 CREATE A PERFECT PARTY PLAYLIST

Hey, DJ! To rock the right tunes at a bash, consider the vibe. A birthday party is a great time to spin upbeat dance tunes and songs playing on the radio right this second. A sleepover can go either way: You and your girls might want to dance like crazy, or maybe an acoustic set will enhance the chill, chatty atmosphere. Just remember that the music isn't all about you, even if it's *your* party. Sometimes it's fun to have your friends RSVP with a tune that matches a theme and then compile a custom playlist. If you hate the song of the moment, but everyone else loves it, why not give it a spin at your pool party? That said, don't be afraid to toss in some old-school hits that everyone secretly adores. Can you feel the love tonight? You bet.

STOP DREADING [WHATEVER]

81

The mind has a funny way of tricking us. Often times, we get it into our heads that something is going to be seriously hard, epically unfun or otherwise a drag. And then the dread sets in and, to top it off, your brain starts to spin wild stories about how terribly it could all go wrong. It can feel nuts, but you don't have to let it take over your precious headspace. Try changing your mind by telling yourself it won't be that bad. Prep yourself for whatever it is (like a big test or a summer job) as best you can, then remind yourself that you're ready and that you can handle whatever challenges come your way. Because you *can*—and the more you tell yourself that, the truer it becomes.

LOVE IT!

Think back to the last thing you were dreading. We bet it wasn't actually as bad as you imagined. Keep that in mind when the next lump of doom arises. Thinking positively helps, and so does asking God to calm your nerves.

TAKE BETTER NOTES IN CLASS

First, start by using your best handwriting. Unreadable chicken scratch won't cut it when test time rolls around. Then work to understand what the teacher is saying and put it in your own words. Simply scrawling whatever she spews doesn't help it sink in as well as when you listen, think, then take note accordingly. And if you don't understand something? Ask her to go over the concept again. Nodding and pretending you get it is useless.

82

BE LESS NERVOUS
AROUND THE BOY YOU LIKE

You finally found a guy who truly grills your cheese, but every time you get around him, you lose your cool? "A girl gets nervous around a boy she likes because she puts him on a pedestal, so every time she's around him she thinks she has to impress him," says Dr. Judy Kuriansky. "Next time you feel rattled, remind yourself of the speech you gave in front of the class. It was only scary while you were thinking about it, but once you got up there and started talking, it became easy, right?" Same diff.

83

SURVIVE A PARTY SOLO

Newsflash: it's actually *fun* to go to a bash alone. You don't have to worry if your BF is having a good time or deal with any friend-group drama. It can feel awkward at first, but just follow our fearless guest tips. Start by offering to help the hostess with something, like bowling up chips or manning the playlist. Next, begin introducing yourself. Be genuine, be sweet and dish out the compliments liberally. And all night? Be a participator. Dance when everyone is dancing, suggest a game if the pace has slowed to a crawl and keep your phone off at all times. If you act as though you're comfortable solo, you absolutely will be. And if you're really having trouble finding someone to chat with? Ask the hostess if there's anyone she thinks you'd hit it off with—many a friendship has been launched at a single party. Get chatting, girl, and you might leave feeling like you knew everyone all along.

FIND THE **BEST JEANS** FOR YOUR BODY

To score your best-ever denim, it's key to follow two rules. First, never pay attention to sizes. Getting hung up on the number means you won't really find your best fit. And second, try on many, many pairs of jeans. So have a great breakfast, head to the mall and then start wading through those blues. We've broken down what to look for, based on your body type.

TALL

With those long legs, you tend to tower, but most styles of jeans look amazing on you. Take note…

- Pants that are high-waisted and flared on the bottom flatter you from the back, while slash pockets (aka the diagonal pockets that cut across your thighs) give the illusion of rounder hips.

- Seek out brands that have longer inseams (36 inches is just right for leggy ladies). Lotsa designers make pants for long 'n' lean ladies, but so do mall stores like Gap and Old Navy. Try 'em on in person for the waist and then buy online for the length if you like 'em!

Zendaya

CURVY

Off-the-rack jeans can be tough for you, as the waist and hips don't always both fit. Find something that works well on your hips and rear, and then have a tailor nip in the waist. Don't forget…

- Straight-leg jeans and pants skim over your curves and lengthen your leg line.

- Opt for a slightly higher waist to help define your middle and avoid the dreaded tummy overhang.

Olivia Holt

PETITE

Luckily, more stores are offering great denim for the mini set these days. But ankle pants are secretly your BFF. Plus…

- Buy pants that sit at your waist, and your legs will look miles long.

- Don't pick pairs that hit at your hips—they shrink your legs, which isn't what you want.

Bella Thorne

PEAR

Dark wash jeans were made for your curves (and look great with almost everything), so seek deep hues and keep in mind…

- Bootcuts are perfect for your bod—the hint of flare plays well with fuller hips.

- Do the finger test when shopping—can you comfortably fit a finger in between your body and the waistband of the pants? If you can't, they're too tight.

HOURGLASS

Your jeans should hug your curves, not just hang off them, so don't fear skinny jeans or trouser pants (they make your waist look super mini). Also…

- Bootcut and flare jeans are fab for you—the extra volume at the ankles balances out your overall outfit.

- Don't fall for straight cuts: The wider legs aren't as flattering on girls with hourglass shapes.

3 CUTE T-SHIRT DIYS
YOU CAN DO IN AN AFTERNOON

Tees might be a staple, but nearly every girl's had the moment when she's looked into her drawers and realized this cotton classic has totally taken over. To shake up your collection, try one (or all) of these funsy DIYs.

1. STRIPE IT UP At the craft store, get some fabric paint (try navy or gold), a spongy paint brush and some blue painter's tape. Lay out your old white tee on a big piece of cardboard. Use a ruler to evenly space your tape down the front of your tee, creating a bunch of horizontal blue lines. Then paint in between the lines so your shirt is covered from top to bottom in alternating blue and painted lines. Let it dry completely. Carefully peel off the tape and unveil your new nautical shirt.

2. CLASSIC TIE DYE This one is fun, easy and a great way to create almost-matching shirts for you and your friends—perfect for charity walks, races or pre-season field hockey pick-up games. Simply stock up on old white tees or tanks, then pick up a tie dye kit at the craft store or Walmart and follow the directions.

3. BACK IN ACTION If you've got a plain, solid-colored tee that you're totally sick of, consider giving its back a makeover. Start by carefully cutting six slits across the back (use a ruler and pencil to ensure they're even). Then pinch the fabric that falls between the slices and wrap a piece of ribbon around it, so the gathered fabric almost looks like a bow. Use a bit of hot glue to hold the ribbon in place. Repeat all the way down the back, until all the slivers are gathered up. Then pop it on over a cami for a girly take on the single-hue top.

OBSESS LESS

Worry. Mull. Fret. Whatever you call it, replaying the same thoughts over and over and over in your head is a fast-track to feeling anxious and unsure. To stop the cycle, make like Princess Elsa from *Frozen* and simply let.it.go. Not just once—repeatedly tell yourself that things are going to be OK and that you're super blessed to have your life (even if it doesn't always seem that way). Talk to God about it, too. Replacing the negative thought pattern with the positive one will retrain your brain, and soon you'll be less likely to ruminate over things you can't control or change. To seal the deal, write down things you love about your life in your journal and remind yourself of them every couple days. Altogether now, let it go!

KEEP YOURSELF SAFE

We don't want to scare you, but it's a big, wide world out there. To keep yourself safe, it's critical to pay attention. Lots of girls spend ton of time texting, listening to music with ear buds in and otherwise generally tuning out. That's fine in your bedroom, but if you're on your own, it can be dangerous to slip into space mode. Just like you always look both ways before you cross the street, always keep your head on the swivel when you're going to and from places. Oh, and as for keeping yourself safe online? Never, ever give out your full name, where you live, your school or your phone number. And never plan to meet anyone you've only encountered on social media, unless your parents have talked with her and her parents and you're going to meet with a group in a public place. Be smart, and be cautious, girl.

MAKE A BIRTHDAY CAKE FROM SCRATCH

We know, we know: Those boxed mixes make it super easy to churn out a confection for your BFF in less than an hour. But with a teensy bit more effort and a dash more patience, you can create a totally homemade cake that will taste better, look prettier and show your friends and fam how much you care. We got this recipe from the author of Faithgirlz! *Best Party Book Ever,* Jessica D'Argenio Waller. Follow her recipe, and then marvel at how easy it was.

BETTER-THAN-BASIC BIRTHDAY CAKE

- ½ cup butter, softened, plus more for the pan
- 1 ½ cups sugar
- 3 eggs
- 2 ¼ cups flour plus more for pan
- Scant (just a little) teaspoon salt
- 3 ½ teaspoons baking powder
- 1 ¼ cups milk (look for 2%)
- 2 teaspoons vanilla extract

FOR FROSTING

- 2 cups powdered sugar
- ½ cup butter, softened
- 1 teaspoon vanilla extract
- 2 tablespoons milk
- 16 oz. rainbow sprinkles

SERVINGS

Makes two 9" round cakes, which you'll layer

DIRECTIONS

1. Preheat oven to 350°F while you butter two 9"-round cake pans. Sprinkle a bit of flour over them, shake to cover evenly and tap out excess. Set aside.

2. Use a stand mixer or hand mixer to cream the butter and sugar together until fluffy. Add the eggs one at a time, beating on medium-low speed.

3. Add the flour, salt, baking powder, milk and vanilla, beating until fully combined. Turn speed up to medium-high and beat for 3 minutes.

4. Pour batter into prepared pans and bake for 25 to 30 minutes, or until top is golden brown and a toothpick inserted in the center comes out clean.

5. While cake bakes, prepare the frosting: Mix all ingredients in a medium bowl until smooth and no lumps remain. If too dry, add more milk.

6. Let cakes cool for 15 minutes, then flip one pan over onto a cutting board and lightly tap the bottom of the pan with the blunt edge of a butter knife. Cake should release from pan onto the cutting board, but if not, let it cool longer. Repeat for the second cake.

7. Place one cake right side up on a cake stand or dinner plate. Spread on a thin layer of icing, then place the second cake directly on top of the first.

8. Cover the entire cake surface with icing.

9. Coat cake entirely in sprinkles, using hands to press them onto the sides of the cake if necessary.

Even super indie chicks fall into the trap of letting their friends and family micromanage everything they do, from always allowing BFFs to pick what they do whenever they hang out to asking their mom to make their lunch or letting her do their laundry until they're 20. Not you. Not anymore. To start being more independent right this minute, take back one task that you've been letting someone else handle. Maybe you'll make your own granola for tomorrow's yogurt or braid your own hair before practice (see #60) or pull together a party outfit without consulting your fashionista friends. And tomorrow? Repeat, until you find yourself participating more in your own life.

90

BE MORE INDEPENDENT (BY TONIGHT)

ADMIT
YOU MADE A MISTAKE

Whoops. You flubbed. Whether it was a little misstep or a major mix-up, the key is not to cover it up. We're not saying you have to tell Mom if you mussed your manicure (obviously). But if you bombed a test or got into some kind of trouble, it's time to 'fess up. But how? Talk to your parents (or whoever it is you're telling, like a coach, etc.) when they have a free minute. Ask if you can talk, and then come right out with it. Apologize, and tell them your plan for how to proceed. If you're unsure, ask for their help so they know you want to grow from your goof. It might seem like everyone is perfect, but part of growing up is making the occasional gaffe and learning from the blunders. And forgiveness is a wonderful thing!

LEARN THREE
CONSTELLATIONS

There's nothing better than looking up at the heavens and seeing nature's own sparklers. On a summer day, head to the library and take out a book on the stars, or google around to find a map of the night sky (or try our fave stargazing app, Night Sky). Then pick out a few clusters that you want to identify. There are the standards—Orion, the Dippers—but it's also fun to find the ones that all your friends don't exactly know, like the Summer Triangle or the Seven Sisters. Then every time you go for a nighttime walk with your fam or camp bunkmates, you can impress 'em with your orienteering skills.

Season's Greetings

Thank You

WRITE IN CALLIGRAPHY

The art of creating curlicued letters looks super posh on everything from birthday invites to postcards. Plus, it's fun to send embellished notes to your buds, just because. To start, pro calligrapher Kerry Scott Grolle recommends getting a sketchbook and a felt pen (those fancy pens with the inkwells might look awesome, but are tough for beginners to master). Then begin collecting inspiration wherever you see it—in magazines, books or out in the world (we recommend taking pics or slipping inspiration into your sketchbook). When you get home, attempt to recreate the letters you see, using your felt pen. It might be helpful to look around for tutorials, either in library books or on Pinterest, but teaching yourself can be fun, too. Then get drawing. "Don't be afraid to practice way more than you think you should," says Kerry. "I had an entire page filled with lowercase *p* simply because it was a tough character for my hand to gracefully recreate. It's also fun to look back on the practice sheets and see how far you've come!" It's all very retro chic.

93

MAKE BETTER DECISIONS

Making the right decision is all about finding the balance between what you want now and what's best for your future. And you can't beat the pro and con list for sussing through your options. Pit the two against each other on a piece of paper, and get scribbling. Then go through both sides and witness the outcome. Still not sure? Make up your mind, and wait 24 hours before telling anyone. When the day is up, assess how you feel. Was it the right choice, or do you wish you could reverse it? The more you practice making your own picks, the easier it gets.

FIND YOUR STUDY STYLE

Pop quiz! How do you learn best? Most girls aren't totally sure, so answer these quickie questions to find out.

1. You wanna show off with a batch of not-from-the-box brownies at next week's Save the Dolphins sweets sale, but baking's not exactly your specialty. You...

A) Hit up foodnetwork.com and watch a how-to video on double fudge bars.

B) Scour the cupboards for the Betty Crocker cookbook, then read each step aloud before you even crack an egg.

C) Grab Grandma—and her blue-ribbon recipe. Teamwork.

D) Throw on an apron and dive right in. So what if the first two batches are a bust? Third time's a charm, right?

2. Your family is heading to Paris for vacay. How do you plan to polish your language skills in time for the trip?

A) Create a slide show with pics—and the pronunciations—of popular Parisian sights, like *La Tour Eiffel*.

B) Download French-language podcasts and listen to 'em before bed and first thing when you get up in the a.m. to really nail those nouns.

C) Enlist your BFF as your French buddy. Have her over once a week to practice *parlez*-ing *français*.

D) Rent French flicks (no subtitles!) and check out fashion mags at the library—this way, you'll teach yourself.

3. Dad's driving you to new bud Cassie's house for a sleepover. How do you direct him there?

A) With landmarks: Go past the plaza, make a left at the school and then turn at the first street past the post office.

B) Call Cass for instructions, then repeat 'em to Pops.

C) Find her address on a your phone's nav, and use point-to-point directions to help Dad get you there.

D) Just wing it. You're pretty sure she lives on Baker Street, but who can really be sure?

4. Your class is taking a trip to the aquarium. As soon as the group walks through the doors, you...

A) Hit up the amphibian room and start reading the bulleted facts and stats on each tank.

B) Listen closely as the tour guide talks about the exotic fish.

C) Head to the hands-on tank. You wanna pet the stingrays.

D) Ignore the tour and roam the building solo. You'd rather see the penguins than the piranhas anyway.

5. Homecoming is almost here! When it's time to hit the dance floor, you will...

A) Watch what everyone else is doing before you join in.

B) Wait until the Cha Cha Slide starts blaring. You won't be sliding to the left 'til the music says so.

C) Wow everyone with your moves while encouraging your crew to get out there with ya.

D) As the saying goes, "Dance like no one's watching."

MOSTLY A'S: THE EYES HAVE IT

You absorb everything visually, so you can't quite grasp a concept unless you actually see it. In class, you need an unobstructed view of your teacher's every move, so snag a seat at the front of class. During lectures, take astute notes, drawing diagrams and charts so you really get the picture. Before a test, make a checklist of everything you've got to cover for the next exam. And rewrite key points over and over, since seeing the words will help you remember them. If you blank on a question at test time, close your eyes and visualize where that info was on your outline—it'll come back to you.

MOSTLY B'S: ALL EARS

You learn through listening. Always alert, you quickly pick up new concepts by hearing someone speak or by reading them aloud. That's why you have to save the gossip for after class—you need to listen to get everything Teach is telling you. Don't be afraid to ask her to repeat anything you may have missed. Before each test, pull together a study group for review to talk out concepts, and come up with short songs for each theory or equation so you can sing 'em to yourself at test time. And read your notes aloud so all of the info sticks.

MOSTLY C'S: ALL ABOUT ACTION

You learn through experience. In addition to listening and watching, you do it yourself. Spark up the super sedentary stuff by volunteering to read chapters out loud or to lead a class demo on whatever it is you're learning. Before an exam, you may want to pop in some gum or listen to tunes while reading textbooks. And give your brain breaks by studying in short chunks of time (try 15 to 20 minute blocks, with a 3-minute rest between). Keep moving and you'll concentrate better.

MOSTLY D'S: SELF-TAUGHT STUDENT

You learn through experimentation. A curious chica, you love to test yourself with trial and error, learning from mistakes as you go. You may prefer to learn by yourself, but you can't snooze through the quarter. Set up a list of goals, like snagging that A in English, then come up with your own ideas on how to make 'em happen. Since you work best on your own, study for exams solo. Create practice quizzes, and flip through flash cards each night before bed. That said, if you have trouble with a concept, call a classmate—don't let your independence get in the way of asking for help. Teaching yourself can be awesome, but it can also take ages to land on the right solution.

PLANT A GARDEN

Scattering some seeds, digging in the dirt and then tending to your tiny plants is amazing for busting stress. On a spring day when you're feeling a little frazzled, take an hour off to plant a mini garden. Then put down a sheet of plastic or some newspaper in a sunny corner of your room and watch the goodies grow.

WHAT YOU'LL NEED: Assorted packets of seeds or starter plants. We recommend lavender, rosemary and chamomile • Potting soil • A pot or planter

WHAT YOU'LL DO: Fill your pot or planter box about half full with potting soil. Follow the planting directions on your seeds or starter plants and tuck them safely underground. Cover with more soil, and then water. Place in a spot where they'll get both sun and shade during the day. Water when the soil gets dry and they'll sprout in no time.

LOVE IT!

Don't have a green thumb? Our plant picks are pretty easy to grow, but if you want to keep it even more low-key, head to the hardware store and pick up some potted succulents. These desert darlings do well practically any-where and are cheap to snap up. We like to group them in threes around a room for a cool vibe.

DIVE INTO A POOL

Make a splash with a perf-every-time dive. First, start by ensuring you're in the deep end and there's no one swimming in your path—never, ever dive into shallow water. (Hint: it helps to check the depth by wading into the water first.) Then stand at the edge of the pool, with your arms over your head and your hands in blades and crossed over each other. Bend your knees and spring off the edge, while arcing your body by tucking your belly in and aiming your hands right for the water (you always want your hands to touch first!). If you don't maintain that almost-rainbow shape, you risk doing a painful belly flop.

REMEMBER: You don't want your dive to go super deep... you want to swim just below the surface and then start kicking to propel yourself up.

GET A **BETTER** REPORT CARD

How do you get better grades when it feels like you're already working way hard? "Study one more hour a night," says straight-A student Christy, an 8th grader in Arizona. "More studying sounds awful, but when I added just one more hour a night to my homework time, I went from a few A's and some B's to all A's." Is it worth it? "You bet. Now I know I can do it, and getting a B means I'm not doing my best."

98

NEGOTIATE
A HIGHER ALLOWANCE

99

After an informal poll, we found that most girls' weekly allowances match their ages. Think of an allowance as a paycheck for services. And like any paycheck you earn, getting a raise not only means doing the job you were hired for to the best of your ability, but going above and beyond. To get more moolah, first have a perfect week of completed responsibilities. Then, at the dinner table Sunday night, subtly point out your flawless week and suggest doing some regular chore or task you recognize needs to be done in exchange for, say, two more bucks a week.

100

GROW
2 INCHES
INSTANTLY

Not only does standing straight make you feel fab, look better and exude unshakable confidence, it can actually help you grow taller. "Stand with your weight centered on both feet, and gently pull your shoulders back and down," says Sophie Bartholemy, a yoga instructor at New York Sports Clubs. "Pull your neck back and up slightly so your head is centered between your shoulders, and slightly lift your chin. Inhale, lifting your chest, and exhale through your mouth without dropping your head." Hey, how's the weather up there?

101

FINISH YOUR HOMEWORK QUICKER

WE ASKED home-school teacher Kristen VanKlootwyk of Santa Cruz, Calif., how she motivates her students (since their only work *is* homework). "Make a to-do list of everything you have due," says Kristen. "Tackle the subjects you like the least at the start so you can check them off your list. Then take a 10-minute break to stretch or eat a snack, but don't leave your work area or you might get distracted. Now all you have left are the subjects you really like, and since that homework is fun to you, you'll finish it faster."

Just one more!

102

FAKE IT 'TIL YA...

Make it big, babe. Whether you wanna land more friends or up your confidence, it's all about acting as though you already have what you're looking for. So smile a lot, believe in yourself and know that you're absolutely on your way to making the team, getting the great grade or upping your friend group. The positive energy that you're radiating will get people noticing...and will improve your own outlook. Even if you aren't having the best day, telling yourself that you're living a blessed life no matter what will bring that grin back to your face. You got this, girl.